A Book of Vintage Designs and Instructions for Making Outdoor Furniture and Other Garden Items.

British Library Cataloguing-in-Publication Data
A catalogue record for this book is available from the
British Library

Making and Restoring Furniture

Furniture is the mass noun for the movable objects intended to support various human activities, such as seating, storing, working and sleeping. Most often, at least in the present day - furniture is the product of a lengthy design process and considered a form of decorative art. In addition to furniture's functional role, it can also serve a symbolic or religious purpose, for instance in churches, temples or shrines. It can be made from many materials, including metal, plastic, and wood, using a variety of techniques, joins and decoration, reflecting the local culture from which it originated. Furniture construction can be extremely technical, or very simple, dependent on the desired end product and skills of the maker.

Numerous courses are available to provide a grounding in furniture making, generally designed to broaden practical (as opposed to art historical) knowledge of materials, tools and design. For the amateur maker, such options can be an extremely useful route into building and restoring their own furniture. Typically, restoring furniture has been seen as a job solely for the trained craftsman, however with the advent of readily available courses, books and online tutorials, it has never been easier to start yourself. Furniture construction and restoration does take a good deal of preparation and persistence, not to mention a keen eye for detail, but can be successfully achieved by any enthusiastic individual.

One of the first things to assess, is what to look out for when purchasing (or evaluating your own) old furniture. As a general rule, if you are restoring furniture yourself, look for older mass-produced items, produced after the mid-nineteenth century. These (with some exceptions) will not have very high values, but are incredibly well made - able to last a long time in the family home. If in doubt, do ask an expert however! One should also be aware, that there are certain more recent styles and designers of furniture which are incredibly rare, for example Art Deco, Arts and Crafts, De Stijl and Bauhaus. Another key thing to look out for are 'dovetail joints'; they are strong and require skill to assemble, and are thereby generally a good sign of a well-constructed piece of furniture. Solid wood or plywood backing, for instance on the back or inside of drawers, are also good indicators of age, as solid wood will generally tell you that it is pre-twentieth century, whereas plywood was only utilised after this date. Perhaps more obviously, inscriptions and manufacturer's stamps can tell the owner a lot about their piece of furniture.

Painting and stencilling wood furniture is probably the most common, and easiest starting activity for the amateur furniture restorer. When finishing wood, it is imperative to first make sure that it has been adequately cleaned, removing any dust, shavings or residue. Subsequently, if there are any obvious damages or dents in the furniture, wood putty or filler should be used to fill the gaps. Imperfections or nail holes on the surface may be filled using wood putty (also called plastic wood;

a substance commonly used to fill nail holes in wood prior to finishing. It is often composed of wood dust combined with a binder that dries and a diluent (thinner), and sometimes, pigment). Filler is normally used for an all over smooth-textured finish, by filling pores in the wood grain. It is used particularly on open grained woods such as oak, mahogany and walnut where building up multiple layers of standard wood finish is ineffective or impractical.

After the furniture is thus smartened, it should then be sanded (without entirely removing the finish) and primed before a base coat of paint is applied. Aerosols will provide a smoother finish than paintbrushes. If stencilling afterwards, make sure that the base colour is completely dry before the final step is embarked upon.

Recovering dining room chairs is another popular activity, involving skills with fabric as well as woodwork - also fashionable is metal furniture restoration. Metal work provides slightly different problems to those of traditional wood and chair restoring; one of the main questions is - do you actually want to make the piece 'as good as new?' Rust and signs of wear can be removed to varying degrees, with many choosing to leave their pieces of furniture worn and torn; achieving 'the industrial look', popular in design circles. This is especially the case for small-scale furniture like lighting, various ornaments such as candlesticks and even larger pieces such as cast-iron beds. If a metal piece is going to be painted, it is imperative to first remove the rust however. This is a time consuming, but ultimately rewarding task to complete, and can be done by a professional for larger objects. Once the metal is rust free, all that remains is to prime and paint! Antiquing effects can also be used, i.e. sanding off layers of paint (of differing colours if the maker prefers) - finished off with a clear protective finish.

Today, British professional furniture makers have self organised into a strong and vibrant community, largely under the organisation 'The Worshipful Company of Furniture Makers', commonly referred to as the Furniture Makers or the Furniture Makers Company. Its motto is 'Straight and Strong'! Members of the Company come from many professions and disciplines, but the common link is that all members on joining must be engaged in or with the UK furnishing industry. Thus the work of the Company is delivered by members with wide ranging professional knowledge and skills in manufacturing, retailing, education, journalism; in fact any aspect of the industry. There are many similar organisations across the globe, as well as in the UK, all seeking to integrate and promote the valuable art that is furniture making. Education is a key factor in such endeavours, and maintaining strong links between professional practitioners, didactic colleges and the amateur maker/restorer is crucial. We hope the reader enjoys this book.

Content Page

A SMALL FRAME

A USEFUL garden frame, five by three feet, is illustrated and described in the following notes.

The cheapest and best timber to use for the whole of the construction, is clean red deal. Tongued and grooved flooring boards, 6 or 7 inches wide, are most suitable for the carcase, and they are so arranged that the front of the frame is made up two boards wide, and the back three boards. This saves sawing and simplifies the construction.

It is usual to frame up the front and back first, and these in turn are screwed to two inch square cleats, kept flush with the ends of the boards. The screws are driven from the face side, 2in. No. 10 is a suitable size screw to use.

The Frame Complete

The boards forming the sides are screwed to the two inch cleats, commencing with the bottom board upon either side. This completes the outer frame with the exception of the 3in. by 1in. boards, nailed upon either side and in the centre.

Those upon the outside of the frame are allowed to project above the frame, equal to the thickness of the lights, say two inches, while the centre one is kept flush with the upper edges, and can be notched in a quarter of an inch for extra strength, to be nailed or screwed through from the outside.

These form the actual runners for the sliding sashes. A part of the completed frame is shown in Fig. 1.

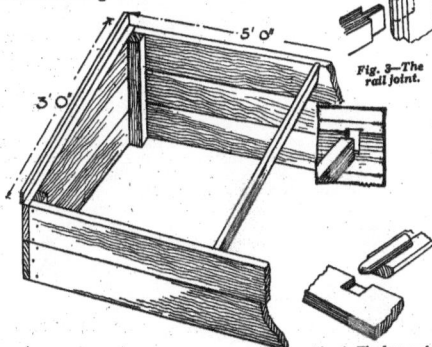

For a frame of this size, it is recommended that two sashes be fitted ; it will be found advantageous in use. These sashes or 'lights' as they are commonly called, can be purchased ready made, or alternatively a secondhand sash can be used, and a frame made to suit. The sizes of the sashes are shown in Fig. 2, which also shows the various joints used in the construction.

In Fig. 3 is shown the joint between top rail and stile, while Fig. 4 shows a suitable method of joining the bars to the apron piece, the joint being further secured by nailing, with one or more oval brads.

Sash stuff, as it is called, can be purchased quite cheaply from a builder's yard, and is ready for use, so it only remains to make the joint to complete the sash.

(Continued on opposite page)

Fig. 3—The rail joint.

Fig. 1—A detail showing construction.

Fig. 4—The bar and apron joint.

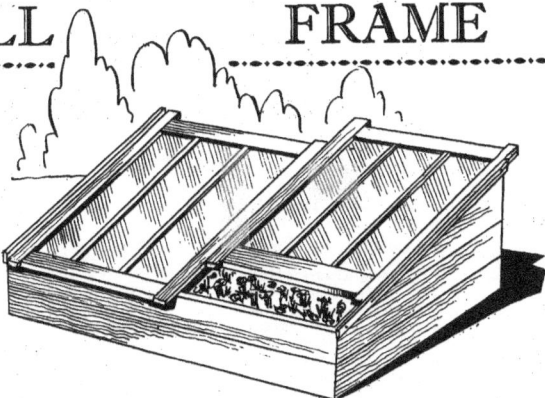

Fig. 2—How to make the sliding sash.

5' 0"

3' 0"

3' 5"

2' 6"

IN many gardens one generally finds a Bird Table adding to their beauty. Placed in an odd corner, amidst a nicely arranged rockery as a background, such a structure as shown in our sketch would, we suggest, add a picturesque note.

Quite a number of the more recent bird houses have their roofs covered with either straw or heather thatch instead of the ordinary wood. The thatch certainly gives a real old-time appearance, it being very simple to put on.

Another item which greatly adds to the beauty is a tree-stump perch fixed to the table at one end.

The House Frame

In making up the table illustrated, the house itself should first be made. The construction of this is shown (Fig. 1), and consists of a plain piece of board for the base 21ins. long by 12ins. or three pieces 4ins. wide. All are ⅛in. thick with uprights of ⅜in. square stuff, 8ins. long. These are built up, being held together at their extremities by two

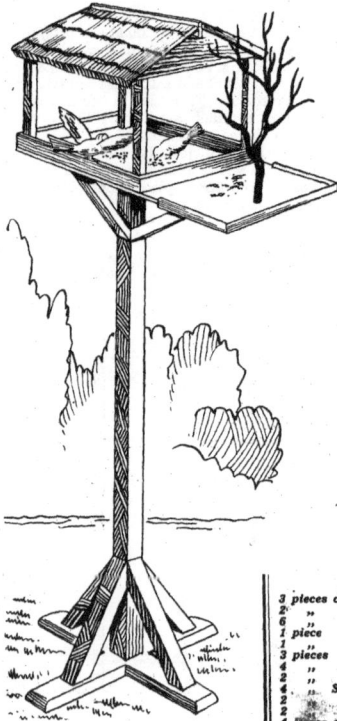

pieces of wood, 15ins. by 1in. by ⅛in. and two pieces 11½ins. by 1in. by ⅛in.

To the top of each upright and facing inwards, are screwed angle plates to hold the gables of wood immediately above. These plates are of brass and can be bought from Hobbies for 5d. the set of four, the number to be quoted when ordering being 101. The enlarged detail (Fig. 1) shows how these are screwed on.

The two gables are of ⅜in. wood, cut to the shape and dimensions shown (Fig. 2.) The notches at the point are cut out to receive the ridge piece which holds the two ends firmly together. This piece is also shown in the figure with the positions dotted on where it fits into the gables.

The Roof Pieces

The ridge itself is of ⅜in. wood. After the end gables and the ridge are fixed, the six boards running the length of the roof are cut and nailed in. Each board is 13¼ins. long by about 1½ins. wide and ⅛in. thick.

Before fixing these boards, get the positions for fixing them by drawing lines ½in. down from the top edges, as shown by the dotted lines (Fig. 2) and the detail (Fig. 3). The larger diagram (Fig. 3) shows the boards fixed and in place, the near gable board being removed for sake of clearness.

The house portion is now complete, except for the thatching, this should be done when all the other work is complete.

The Pole Support

The pole is of 2ins. square stuff and cut to any desired length not greater than 5 feet. The feet to which the pole is fixed are made up (see Fig. 4) from two pieces of board 2 feet long, halved together in the middle. The boards are 3ins. wide and ⅜in. thick, and the halvings made after careful marking out with a tenon saw and chisel.

Square the lines across accurately before cutting, when these are together they should have all angles rectangular.

Fix them by means of two stout screws at diagonal corners, indicated, room being left for a long screw to pass upwards into the pole. After the foot has been so fixed, proceed to make the sloping supports, these are of 2in. by ⅜in. stuff with the ends cut to 45° to fit between foot and post.

Take care to bore the holes for the nails which fix these supports or the wood will be sure to

Garden Bird Table—*(continued)*

split in driving them home. Bore a hole in the baseboard of the house and run a good long screw down through it into the post.

Underneath the board there are four bracket pieces. The one immediately beneath the projecting front has its ends cut to a 45° angle, the other three must be cut roughly to length, then laid in place against the post and board, the angles thus made being marked off and cut. The lengths of the brackets are suggested (Fig. 5). These are 2ins. wide and ½in. thick. Here again the holes for the nails for fixing must be bored to avoid splitting the wood.

the twig-wood should be added to each side slope.

If the thatch is to be of heather, these should be in small bundles tied up with grass and laid on, copper tacks being run in to hold it well down. Trim the ragged ends off with garden hand shears.

Wood for making this Bird Table may be bought from Hobbies Ltd. Special strips of satin walnut are included for certain parts of the house, such as the ⅜in. square uprights and the rail that goes round them. All other parts are of deal and the whole should be coated with creosote or other wood preservative. If preferred, a green and brown paint may be applied.

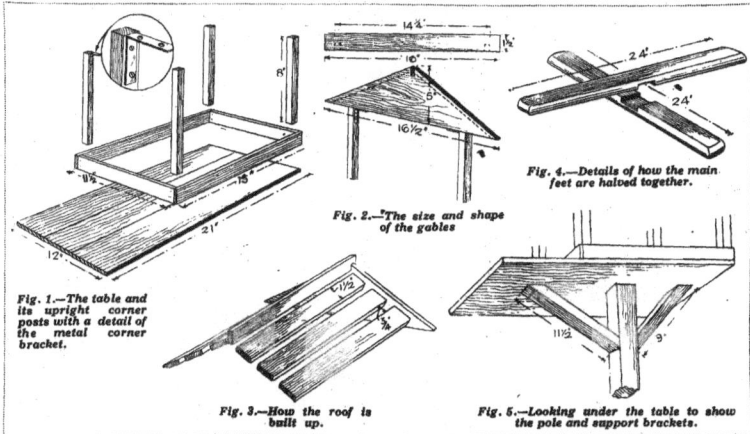

Fig. 1.—The table and its upright corner posts with a detail of the metal corner bracket.

Fig. 2.—The size and shape of the gables

Fig. 3.—How the roof is built up.

Fig. 4.—Details of how the main feet are halved together.

Fig. 5.—Looking under the table to show the pole and support brackets.

Note that there will be three bracket pieces 9ins. long and only one 11½ins. The two side 9in. brackets have been omitted from the sketch (Fig. 5) for sake of clearness in detail.

The table is now more or less finished and it only remains to add the thatching. If this is to be of straw, a quantity of good straight stuff should be chosen and cut to length to meet at the ridge and to overhang slightly at the lower edge or eaves of the house.

Some pieces of twig, cut the same length as the ridge, are laid over the straw thatch and tacked down with long copper tacks. Three strands of

The main post of 2in. square stuff has not been included in the price of the wood, it being thought best to get this locally. Some workers may have the post let into the ground instead of being fixed to cross feet as shown.

The price of the wood is 2/- (plus 1/- postage) and when ordered Parcel No. T.M. 295 should be asked for.

12ins. being rather wide for ordinary deal wood, it will be found that the pieces put up in the parcel are 4ins. wide, small strips of odd wood being nailed underneath to clamp them together to make the full width of 12ins.

A NOVEL GARDEN BARROW

HERE is a useful and novel garden appliance for keeping the lawn and garden clear of leaves and rubbish. It is, as the sketch shows, a container on wheels which is easily pushed about and turned round in any desired position while gathering up unwanted rubbish.

The box or container is made of ⅜in. wood to the measurements given (Fig. 1). It must be noticed that the back of the box —that part to which the handle and the axle of the wheel is fixed, is a square cut piece 15ins. long by 9ins. wide, whereas the sides are cut to a taper from 9ins. at the top to 7ins. at the bottom.

The front also is cut square, same as the back, only it is ½in. longer to allow for the taper of sides. Notice that the sides go in between the front and the back, nails or screws being used for fixing. Take careful measurements for the floor piece which will drop in and then nailed to sides, front, etc., as shown (Fig. 2). Clean off with coarse glasspaper the sharp edges of the box or just plane if desired.

Two first-class wheels for the article may be got from Hobbies for 8d., these are of hardwood, nicely turned and bored ready for the stout screws

and washers which are supplied with the wheels. The axle to take these wheels consists of a piece of stuff 11ins. long by 1¼ins. by ¾in. and fixed to the base of the box with three stout countersunk screws (Fig. 3).

Do not put the wheels on until after all the other work has been done. The stump foot supporting the box when at rest, consists simply of a piece of deal about 6ins. long, 2ins. wide and ½in. thick, cut to the shape shown in the detail (Fig. 2) and fixed with two screws. The corners and sharp edges should be cleaned off.

The length of the handle is suggested as 24ins., this being varied to suit. It is of 1¼ins. by ¾in. stuff and simply screwed to the top portion of the box (Fig. 3). At the top of this handle piece is fitted a cross arm for ease in manipulating the wheels.

The cross arm is shown (Fig. 4) marked off and with a recess cut in the middle to hold firmly to the upright. It is of 1¼ins. by ¾in. stuff. The hand grips of this piece are rounded off with a rasp and smoothed up with coarse and fine glass-paper.

A very useful addition to the box

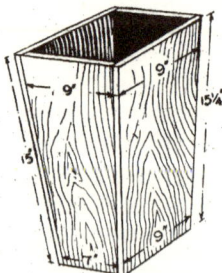

Fig. 1.—The main box framework.

Fig. 2.—A general picture of the construction.

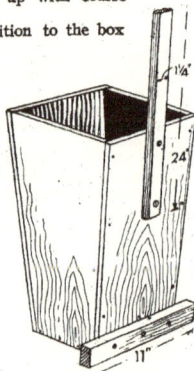

Fig. 3.—The handle upright and wheel axle.

A Garden Barrow—(continued)

is the tool rack along the front. This consists simply of two shaped ends cut as the enlarged detail shows from ⅜in. stuff and screwed on from inside the box about 5 or 6ins. down from the top edge. To the front of these pieces again is screwed a plain piece about 8ins. long by 2ins. wide and ½in. thick.

It will be found when this rack is finished that such small garden tools as the hand trowel and fork fit well into it and are always at hand when required. A weed lifter for picking weeds from a grass lawn would also be easily carried.

The completed box should be glasspapered up and then coated with some wood preservative such as creosote or a good green stain given with a coating of varnish would look attractive. Two coats of green paint being most serviceable.

We print a cutting list of wood required for making up the garden barrow, this should prove most useful when ordering. The wheels as before stated may be got from Hobbies Ltd. together with the screws and washers.

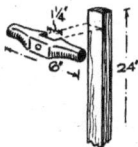

Making the handle.

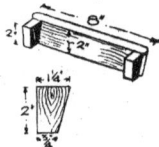

The tool rack.

A FOLDING CHAIR

As a suggestion, why not make a folding chair in your spare time?

It will have many uses, and at the least is very convenient in the garden during the summer. We give a table of materials which are required to make a light folding chair of simple design and construction. The drawings which are also given, when taken with the table of requirements, are self explanatory, and do not make it necessary to go closely into det

One or two items will, howeve instance, the seat and back rest are made of canvas, the ends of the back rest having pockets provided for the purpose of slipping onto the two inclined pieces which extend from the back legs.

The method employed is to mortice and tenon all the fixed joints; the connections which allow the folding of the chair to take place, were made of thick round wire nails riveted over washers, and four hoop iron strips likewise riveted.

Softwood, white or red deal, is the best to use for constructing the chair, and it may be finished with stain, or gluesize and varnish.

MATᵀᴾIALS REQUIRED

		Wood	
	No. of Pieces	*Sizes in inches*	*Length in inches*
Legs	4	2 by 1	27
Arms	2	2 by 1	21
Lower Rails ..	2	2 by 1	18
Slats	6	1 by ½	14
Backs	2	2 by 1	16
Cross Pieces ..	4	1½ by ¾	26½
Seat Rails ..	2	1½ by 1	18
Packing Pieces ..	2	2 by ¼	5
		Metal	
Link Straps ..	4	¾ by 1/16	6
Stirrup Straps ..	2	¾ by 1/16	10
Rivet Pins.. ..	4	¼ round	3
,, ...	4	¼ round	2½
,, ...	2	¼ round	2
,, ...	4	¼ round	1½
Back ..		1 piece of canvas	32 by
Seat ..		1 ,, ,,	26 by

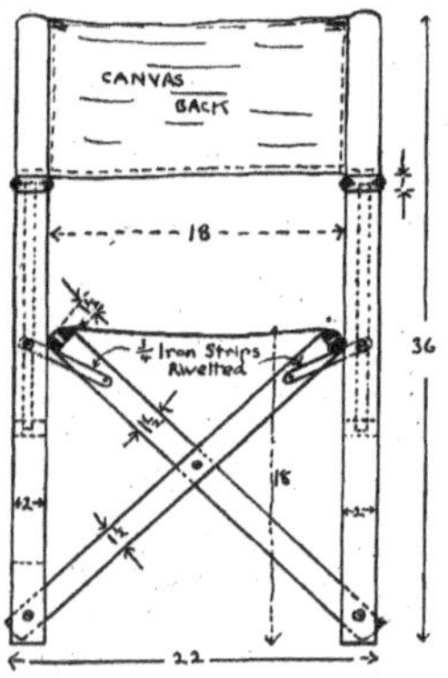

CANVAS
BACK
18
Iron Strips Rivetted
36
18
22

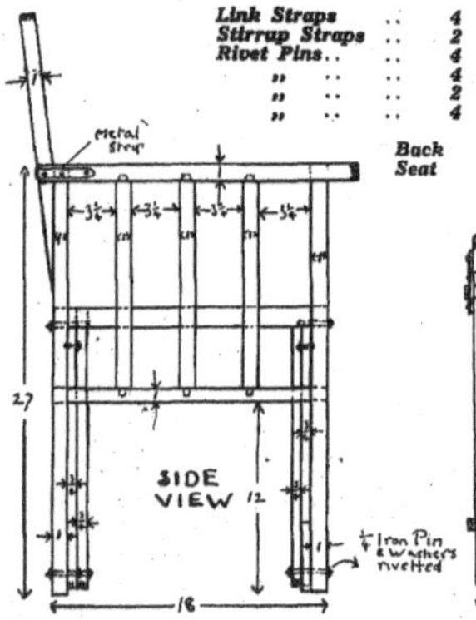

Metal Strap
27
SIDE VIEW
Iron Pin & Washers rivetted
18

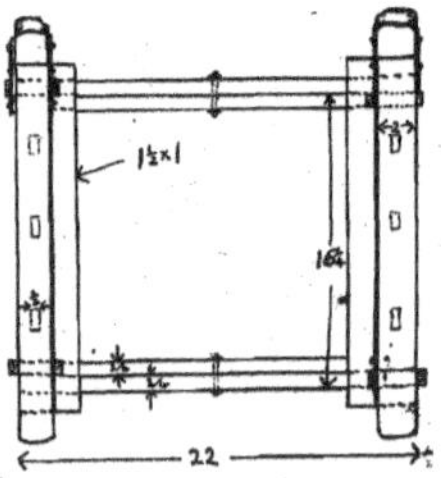

1½x1
22

A TEA WAGON
FOR THE GARDEN

THE simple little trolley shown in our sketch would be suitable for use for afternoon tea on the lawn, or for indoor use in the winter time. The construction is of the simplest, and there are no difficult joints to mark out and cut.

The cost, too, is very small as ordinary deal or pine can be used throughout, except for the tray top which consists of 3/16in. plywood.

The best finish for the wood is a cellulose paint as it is quite easy to put on and gives a smooth hard surface.

The size of the tray itself is 21½ins. long by 14½ins. wide and the height from the ground to top is 2 feet. It has two wheels only which make smooth running when held by the handle on the opposite end.

The Framework

At Fig. 1 is a useful and fully dimensioned side view of the trolley and a good deal of the setting out of the parts can be got from this. The two main legs are 2 ft. long and the two shorter ones (to which the wheels are attached) 1ft. 10¾ins. long. All are of 1in. square wood.

The tops are held together by four rails 1½in. wide by ⅜in. thick, the long side ones being 22ins. long while the shorter ones are 14½ins. long. At Fig. 2 is shown how the long side rails are let into the tops of the legs and nailed or screwed to them,

the shorter rails being simply fixed flush on the faces of the legs. The larger diagram in the circle clearly shows how the tops of the legs are cut out to receive the rails.

If the framework needs additional stiffening while it is being put together, small blocks of wood may be screwed into the corners between the rails and the legs, but it is not advisable or necessary to make the top unduly heavy by adding heavy blocks.

The Rails

At a distance of 16ins. from the underside of the top rails, two lower side rails are fixed. These are also let into the legs as shown in Fig. 3 where A shows how the recesses are marked and cut, and B one of the rails screwed in place. These lower rails are 1½ins. wide and ⅜in. thick, and are countersunk screwed to the legs.

Connecting these two side rails are three cross rails 16ins. long by 1¼ins. wide and ⅜in. thick. They are (Fig. 1) spaced 1in. in from the legs at each end and 6⅜ins. apart. These rails not only strengthen the trolley at this part, but they form a very useful rest upon which to put a tray or large plates.

The Top

The top may now be made and fixed. A piece of 3/16in. plywood 1ft. 10ins. by 15ins. is cut square and fitted over and screwed to the top rails (see Fig. 4). When the plywood is securely fixed, the four edges should be cleaned round with a rasp and glasspaper and the side ledges then measured for and cut. The edging strips or ledges are 1⅛ins. wide and ⅜in. thick and the top edges should be rounded off with plane and glasspaper as the enlarged detail shows in Fig. 1. The strips are mitred at the corners and are fixed to the rails with round-headed brass screws. The projection of the ledges above the plywood top should not be less than ⅝in.

The forward corner of the plywood top in Fig. 4 has been cut away to show how it fits on the rails. For the handle, two pieces of ⅜in. wood marked out

The completed Trolley

11

Tea Wagon—*(continued)*

and cut as in Fig. 5 are required. First mark and cut out one and then use this for marking round as a template for the second one. Clean round the edges with glasspaper and screw them to the insides of the legs as given in the detail in Fig. 5.

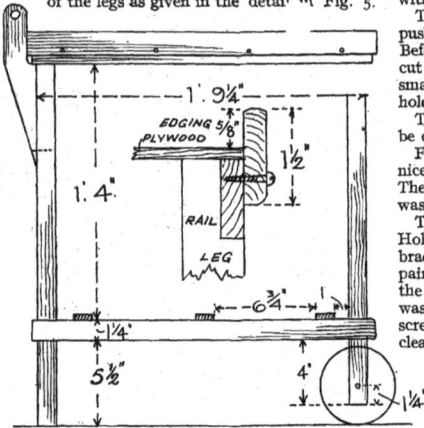

Fig. 1—A side view with dimensions of parts.

Countersink the holes before the screws are put in and fill the heads with prepared stopping.

Note from Fig. 5 that the handles butt up flush with the lower edges of the top rails and stand level with the backs or insides of the legs.

The handle bar is a length of ½in. dowel rod pushed through the two holes in the uprights. Before being pushed through, however, a shallow cut should be made in each end so when in place small thin wafers or wedges can be driven in to hold the bar tight.

The cleaning and finishing with paint should now be done and the wheels finally screwed on.

For the latter, Hobbies can supply a pair of nicely turned hardwood wheels for 8d. (No. 604). They are 5ins. in diameter and the screws and washers for fixing are supplied with them.

The position for the screws is indicated in Fig. 1. Holes should be bored about ½in. deep with a small bradawl 1½ins. from the lower end of the short pair of legs. A washer is placed over the hole and the screws put through the wheel. A second washer is, of course, added at the large end of the screw before the wheel is put on. Leave sufficient clearance for the wheels to turn freely.

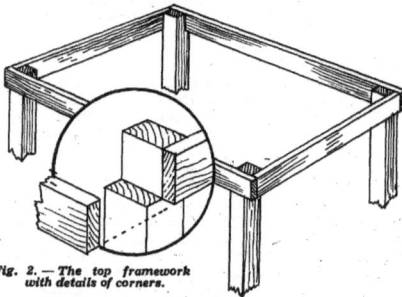

Fig. 2. — The top framework with details of corners.

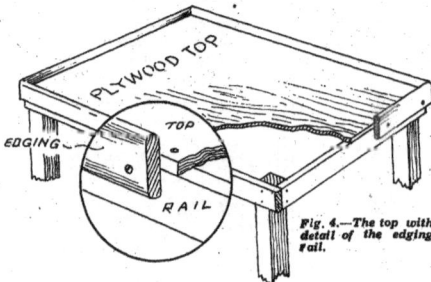

Fig. 3. — How the lower cross rails are let into the legs.

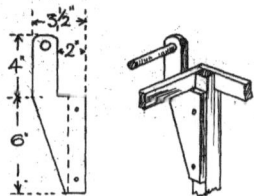

Fig. 4.—The top with detail of the edging rail.

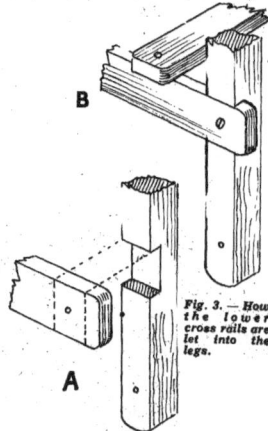

Fig. 5.—Details of the handle parts.

AN ELECTRIC WIND DIRECTION INDICATOR

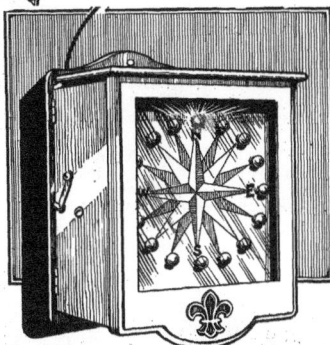

Although intended mainly for Scouts, this design is a novelty anyone can make. All patterns are on Design Sheet No. 2086.

HERE is an electrical novelty which tells you at a glance from which direction the wind is blowing. It lights a lamp and shows you on the compass the exact point. The illustration gives a good idea of the finished article.

It is particularly helpful to all in the Scout movement, and has been specially planned so troops can make one to fit up in their headquarters or den. It is a combination of woodwork and electrical apparatus which indicates the direction of the wind by means of lighting up bulbs on the various points of the compass.

The weathervane on the roof actuates a current, and when the switch is turned on, contact is made with the various points of the compass shown in the cabinet hanging on the wall. As the vane swings to and fro, the light alters and shows exactly the direction from which the wind comes.

In Two Portions

The illustration, of course, is concentrated, because really the box with the electrical bulbs in, hangs on the wall in the den or clubroom, whilst the mechanism is in the false roof just above the ceiling, and the final connection is with the weathervane through the top.

We are mainly concerned with the building of the box and spindle holder, as the wiring is a straightforward matter which most amateur electricians can undertake. The pattern sheet shows clearly the parts required, but a careful study should be made of them to know how the two parts should be made up.

All of it is in plain fretwood, and a parcel is supplied as usual by Hobbies Ltd. Get out the various pieces first, cut them with the fretsaw and clean off all the paper remains. In this respect, note that the pattern of the actual dial is left on the wood, and can be painted in later more attractively with water colours or enamel.

The back of the main box is hung to the wall by a keyhole on the lid, and on to the front of this is hinged the hollow framework of the sides, top, bottom and front. The floor goes between the sides, but the top rests on the edges of the sides and projects slightly beyond.

It will be a good plan, by the way, to get a second copy of Hobbies Weekly so the constructional details shown on the various parts can be seen on the second design sheet after the first has been used and the various parts cleaned up. Dotted lines indicate the position of adjoining pieces, and sectional drawings show how they are built up.

On the floor of the box as can be seen by the back view detail, there are two little battery supports. Have the battery at hand which you are going to use, and see these supports are glued to the floor just the right width to hold it firmly.

The pattern of the top must be extended so it measures 6¾ins. as shown by the arrows, and in one corner only has to be taken out a short segment. This segment is necessary to allow the whole thing to swing open on to the back. The semi-circle which has also to be cut in this top piece is to allow for the flex leads to pass out to the other portion of the apparatus.

The Front

The actual front of the dial box is made of three pieces. One is cut to the outline provided by the solid line on the sheet, and the other two are the shape indicated by the dotted lines.

The pattern can quite easily be laid on to the boards, pricked off at the corners and then marked out with a pencil ready for cutting. All three are in ¼in. wood. The smaller pieces are glued one each side of the larger piece which holds the glass in place, as shown by the drawing, at Fig. 1. This glass is also supplied by Hobbies Ltd.

The front completed should be screwed on the framework of the sides, but not glued because it

MATERIALS SUPPLIED

For making this model we supply a parcel of Satin Walnut, etc. for 2/6, post free 3/-. The Fittings include 16 round-head brass screws ¾ in. No. 6; 1 ditto 1¼in. No. 6; 1 pair heavy brass hinges, 1 glass (No. 5805), 1 pair brass hooks and eyes and 5ins. of ⅜in. brass strip. Complete 1/2 per set, or 1/6 post free.

Wind Indicator—(*continued*)

may be necessary to take it off again some time or other. Beneath the glass, by the way, is added the little overlay of the Scout badge, a drawing of which is printed. If you like to add the name of your own Patrol or Troop each side of the badge, it will certainly add to the effectiveness of the whole thing.

The piece showing the compass points is fixed inside the box and set back ⅜in. from the front edge. To allow this, two long strips must be glued along the floor and on the underside of the top ⅜in. inwards, as can also be seen in Fig. 1. These strips take the dial front which is screwed in place.

It is this dial which has the 16 holes showing the various compass points. These holes are drilled exactly the size to take the electric

Fig. 1—A cut-away view of the box.

bulbs. They should fit in tightly, and when in place a flexible wire is turned round each, carried from one to the other the whole of the circle, finally leading off to the switch which is arranged on the side, as can be seen in Fig. 2.

In addition to the wire making the connection round the circle of bulbs,

Fig. 2—Connections behind the compass points.

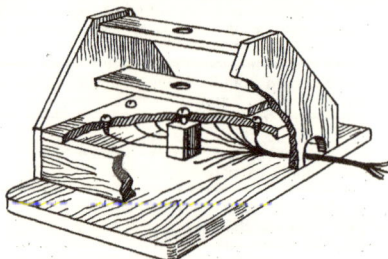

a single wire must be soldered to the back of each, in order to lead up to the vane box above. Each one of these must be cotton covered to keep it insulated, and then all of them can be turned together to lead up as a single cord through the top up to the vane box above.

It will be necessary, by the way, to know first exactly how much of this wire will be required, because the length of it must be allowed for to reach up to the vane box in the ceiling, or wherever it is put.

The Switch

Now have a glance at Fig. 2 and notice how the switch is fixed to the side. This consists of a screw forming a stud to which the wire forming the contact round the bulbs, is fixed, and represents the " on " position. The switch is a simple lever

of brass screwed at one end, and resting on another screw stud at the other. A little shaped handle can be added so the switch can be turned across to " on " and " off " as required.

Some workers may prefer to get the little cheap switches from Woolworth's, and to wire it up neatly in a proper electrical fashion ; whilst others may like to carry the connections just through the side of the box and have the switch on the outside so it is more accessible.

The leads from each of the bulbs have been carried to the vane box. This box is shown in detail on the sheet, and the construction is quite clear from that. A further detail of it is given at Fig. 3, which is a cut-away view showing the wires leading in and fixed up to their respective studs. Round-headed screws form all these connecting studs, and the wire should be soldered on to the underside.

The Contact

On the top we have a piece of spring brass, bent slightly and carried to a centre spindle. This spindle should be of metal, and the top end of it is secured to the weather vane holder. The spindle itself rests upon a round-head screw in the centre of the platform, which is slightly raised by a support block glued on.

This spindle should have as little friction as possible, because it must turn as the wind blows the vane round. The arm of the spindle is the strip which connects to each of the screws indicating the point of the compass. This brass strip should be sufficiently springy to make good contact as it passes round, and yet not sufficient to prevent the vane turning comfortably.

It will be a good plan to work out all the connections first, and

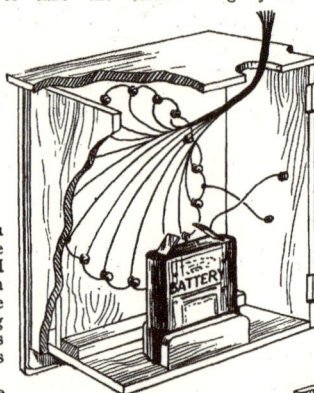

Fig. 3—The connections in the vane box.

remember to get the connection for the bulb at the north, with the same stud in the vane box. This can be done by trial. Test each wire with a conecting stud in the vane box, and make a note

Wind Indicator—

of the one which lights up the north compass point when the vane is from that direction. Then work round each of the other points, and connect them properly to their respective studs.

Do not, of course, attempt to fix the apparatus until you are sure you have got everything correct. Little things can be added as required. The box, for instance, opens and closes on to the back hanging on the wall. It must be fitted with two little catches on one side, which hold it when shut. See, too, that it opens and closes with ease.

Having got the connections right, make up your mind to add a switch on the outside as mentioned. Be sure that none of the leads is faulty or shorts across to another one. A wiring circuit for the whole thing is given on the design sheet, which clearly shows the connections. Remember to get a battery of the same voltage as your lights, or you will blow the bulbs every time.

Do not leave the switch on unnecessarily or the battery will run down and be no use when required.

The whole apparatus can be finished with a coat of polish put on with a brush, but remember to have the box open when doing this, so the parts do not stick together with the polish. Or, of course, the whole thing could be painted in the troop colours.

The making of such an electrical apparatus forms an interesting and fascinating piece of work, which can be undertaken by any Scout, and is certainly an addition worth while for any headquarters or clubroom.

Make up your mind to have it complete this month, so you will be ready to start on the next Scout design when it comes along.

Here is an everyday job for the handyman with a few carpentry tools. If required, the complete lot of boards can be obtained from Hobbies Ltd. (Parcel No. 265), for 5/- carriage forward.

The Roof Recesses

A centre line should next be erected on the boards and 23ins set up upon this with a height of 18ins. at each side edge as given in Fig. 1. Connect up these points and then saw through to get the pointed end of the gable.

Next mark out the recesses in the sloping edges which are to take the roof battens. Each recess is 2ins. long and ⅜ins. deep and set out as shown in the example. Cut down vertically with the tenon saw and chisel away the waste wood between the cuts. The other gable end is made up exactly similar to this one, in fact, after having nailed up the four boards with their cross rails, the finished one may be laid on this and marked round exactly and cut and planed down.

The Entrance

One end must now have an opening cut in it to the size shown, the wood being sawn away either with a coarse fretsaw or a keyhole saw. The opening so made should be thoroughly glass-papered and all sharp edges or splinters of wood taken off.

The two sides of the kennel are each made up of six pieces of matching knocked together and held by two rails placed as shown in Fig. 2. The rails are cut from matching sawn down the centre and the tongue and groove of the piece planed away.

Fitting and Fixing

Care should be taken to closely nail each end board as shown, so that when the rails are cut across short at the ends, sufficient strength is left to hold them well to the rails. A piece 1½ins. long is cut from the ends of the rails from the gable ends to fit in and lie flush.

THE illustration given shows a very cosy type of kennel. It has a projecting roof at the front which affords good shelter from rain and wind, whilst a removable floor (to which the house may be hinged if desired), makes for ease in cleaning. The kennel is made up from seven distinct sections consisting of two gable ends, two sides, two roof slopes and a base.

Kennel length is 30ins., and width 20ins. with side height measurement of 18ins., and match-boarding ⅜in. in thickness used throughout.

The First Job

A start should be made with the ends, or gables, shown at Fig. 1 and for each gable four pieces of matchboard 5¾ins. wide and 24ins. long are tapped together and narrow cross rails nailed on as shown. The one along the lower end of the gable is flush with the edge of the boards and another 15ins. up from this.

The total width measuring about 22ins. and along one edge a projecting tongue is left, while the corresponding edge carries a groove. Both tongue and groove must be planed away, and each edge got down until a width of 20ins. remains.

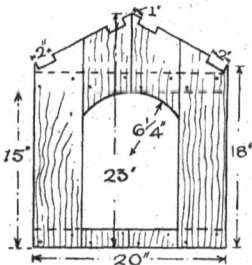

Fig. 1—Details and dimensions of the parts forming the front.

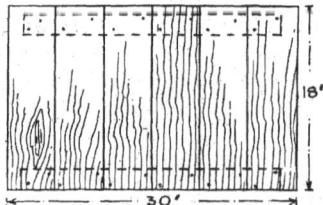

Fig. 2—How the side is made up of six boards.

Making a Dog Kennel—(continued)

The method of fitting and fixing the sides and ends is shown in Fig. 3, the enlarged diagram showing in detail how the ends fit in between the sides. All the parts should be screwed together with round headed brass screws, no glue of course being used at all. The top edge of each side must be planed away to a chamfer to allow the roof to lie flat, the lines of the chamfer corresponding with the slopes of the gable. Figure 4 shows the four sections of the kennel erected and ready to be fitted to the base. The last section being made before the roof slopes are put in hand.

The construction of the base is given in Fig. 5, and for this eight pieces of matching must be cut 24ins. long and tapped together.

The Edge Rails

Two edge-on rails are cut to the

each rail, with perhaps an additional rail along the centre if it is found advisable. Plane up all the exposed edges and finish with glasspaper.

The construction of one of the roof slopes with the necessary measurements is given in Fig. 6.

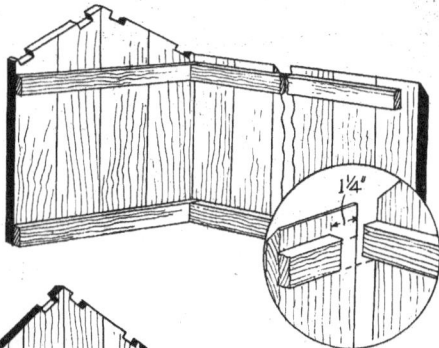

Fig. 3—The end and side with detail of the joint between.

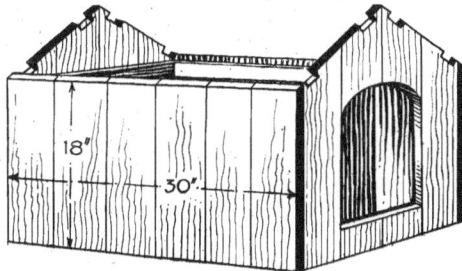

Fig. 4—The framework of the kennel ready for the base.

CUTTING LIST

All ⅞in. Matchboard-ing, 5⅞ins. wide, except rails, which are to be of 1in. stuff.
8 pieces 24ins. long.
12 pieces 18ins. long.
16 pieces 15ins. long.
2 pieces 21ins. long.
2 pieces 30ins. long.
2 pieces 42ins. long.
8 pieces 24ins. long.
1 piece 42ins. long.
4ins. wide, 1in. thick.

---

required length, and the necessary cutting off, planing away of the groove at one end, and the tongue at the other end of the platform again done.

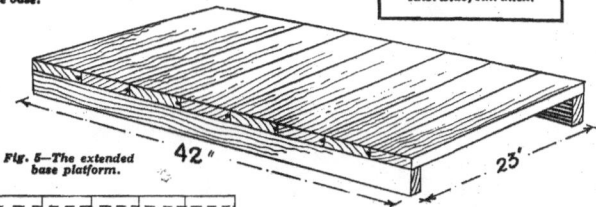

Fig. 5—The extended base platform.

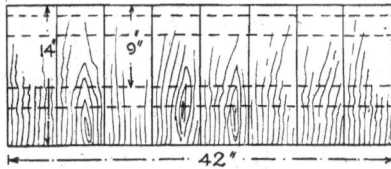

Fig. 6—The roof slopes with a dotted line to show position of the cross rails.

The edging rails must be of thicker stuff than the ⅞in. matching wood, at least 1in. being used for

Here again eight pieces are cut to length and nailed to narrow rails, running only the whole length and not being cut off short as were the rails for the sides of the kennel. The spacing of the rails should be checked with the recesses made in the gable ends, as it is in these recesses that they will ultimately rest. The top edges of each section must be chamfered to meet at a point. After testing the fit of each, the piece is be fixed to the gables with screws.

Some workers may choose to nail a piece of round ridge, having a V cut in it, to fit over the

Making a Dog Kennel—*(continued)*

roof slopes to the boards to make a really satisfactory watertight job. This ridging can be bought shaped and moulded, quite cheaply, from any local builder.

A pair of stout hinges should be screwed to one side of the kennel and to the base. The former can then be turned over on its side to facilitate interior cleansing.

Regarding the finish to be adopted for the outside, either a priming coat and two coats of good paint should be given, or the whole may be gone over with creosote. The underside of the base receiving a double coating of this preservative.

The roof slopes would look well and effectively weatherproofed by the addition of either Ruberoid or a covering of ordinary linoleum painted over.

Jobs about the House

A NEATLY made box fitted inside the front door of the house is a desirable fitment that any handyman can make, as a receptacle for incoming mail.

It is sometimes considered that such a letter box is more readily accessible to pilferers, but this objection is overcome by making the box sufficiently deep and providing it with a rounded top.

Both these conditions conduce to a neat and shapely appearance, a matter that is worth bearing in mind as the box is constantly under the eyes of all visitors.

Wood to Use

Good clean deal about ⅜in. to ½in. in thickness is a suitable material with which to make the box, although it can be constructed with American whitewood, oak, or mahogany if preferred. The general appearance of the finished article is seen in Fig. 1, which also shows the inner door opened to give access to the letters.

Each individual piece is shown separately in Fig. 2, which will serve to give the proper proportions, dimensions are not shown as they must necessarily be adapted to accord with individual requirements.

The back (A) should have the grain of the wood running vertically and the slot for the letters should be of a size that just corresponds with the opening in the door.

The two side pieces (B and C) should also have the grain vertical, and must be sawn off at the upper part to curve as shown. Care must be taken to make both pieces exactly alike in all respects and perfectly square on all edges and at the lower corners.

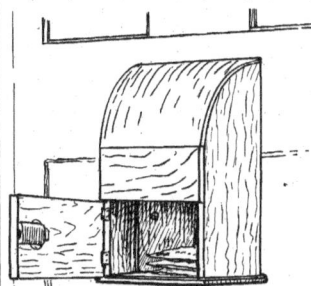

Fig. 1—The box fixed to the door.

The bottom (D), top (E) the fixed board (F) and the door (G) should have the grain running in the direction of greatest length, as should be the case with the bottom board (D). The width of the top, the fixed board and of the door, should exactly equal that of the backboard (A) but the bottom may be a trifle wider and longer to allow of rounding off the edges to impart a smarter and more workmanlike appearance.

Gluing the Framework

Prepare all these pieces by planing them smooth, if they have not been bought from Hobbies Ltd., on both faces and square on all edges. Then glue the back edges of the side pieces and stand them upright on the workbench, with the glued edges uppermost. Place the backboard upon them and secure the joint with a few panel pins. Turn the structure upside down and similarly fit the fixed board to the outer edges.

Then glue the bottom board into place and fasten it with a few thin screws about 1½ins. long. Similarly screw the other pieces and take care to countersink all the screw holes so that the screw heads sink below the surface.

This stage of the work is pictured in Fig. 3, and the succeeding operation is to plane off the upper edges of the fixed board and the backboard to the same angle as the side pieces.

Fitting the Door

Tack the top board which should be of 1/32nd in. plywood, temporarily in place and plane off the front and back edges to correspond with the front and back faces of the box. The door should then be fitted so it exactly fills the space between the lower edge of the fixed board and of the bottom board and is flush at both sides.

This being done, the door can be hinged at the right or left hand side to the edge of side piece, using good long narrow

Fig. 3—The box part assembled.

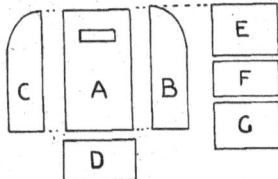

Fig. 2—The shapes of all parts.

C | A | B

D

E

F

G

Fitting a Letter Box—*(continued)*

hinges which are generally known as cabinet hinges. Then procure a strong cupboard lock and fix it to the inside of the door with short thick round-headed screws.

Mark the position for the keyhole and proceed to cut it ; for which purpose, drill a hole through the door in line with that of the lock, and saw or file away the wood to clear the key.

Fix a neat escutcheon plate over the aperture, then close the door and endeavour to lock it. This will cause the bolt to make a slight mark on the inner edge of the side piece and will show just where to cut the slot. It is generally necessary to fit a slotted metal plate over the hole in the wood

to ensure security and long life. When the lock works nicely, give the wood a rub down with sandpaper and then apply a coat of woodfiller. Allow this to dry, again sandpaper the box and give it a coat of stain, or of flat oil colour.

Then screw the box to the back of the door, using screws at the top and at the bottom driving the screws through the opened doorway.

Finally, complete the staining and varnishing—or the painting and enamelling as the case may be—while the box is in place. If desired, the door could be made with picture frame moulding and the opening glazed in the usual way, giving visible evidence of the presence of letters within the box.

www.ingramcontent.com/pod-product-compliance
Lightning Source LLC
Chambersburg PA
CBHW031009090426
42737CB00008B/750